ENGAGE EVERY DAY!

David Zinger

People Artists

Drawing Out the Best in Others at Work

Peter W. Hart and David Zinger

Foreword

In this age of wars for talent and hyper competition, the impact of leadership is being scrutinized more than ever as organizations grapple with how to link leadership effectiveness with a company's key performance indicators. This is a question that organizational scientists have examined in thousands of studies over the past 100 years. The evidence from these studies of leadership is clear: Leaders can have a tremendous influence on the thoughts, feelings, and actions of their employees. The flipside of this question for the leaders on the ground is how should they best wield this influence? The question has been vexing because there is an overabundance of advice from a variety of sources and it is unlikely that there is one "correct" answer.

People Artistry represents a unique and humanistic response to this question. Its message is to find your own way of meaningfully and authentically connecting and building relationships with your employees. The examples and stories this book contains offer ideas and suggestions about how to make those meaningful connections and bring out the best in your employees (and maybe yourself along the way). For managers looking to build and maintain authentic and sustainable relationships that bring out the best in others, this book offers pragmatic and inspirational ideas for becoming a People Artist.

Dr. Charles Scherbaum
Associate Professor of Psychology
Baruch College, City University of New York

Preface

Peter W. Hart is the CEO of Rideau in Montreal, Canada. Rideau originated in 1912 and currently has 250 employees providing corporate and government recognition solutions around the globe.

Peter Hart is also an artist with a gallery in the Old Port of Montreal. Peter's art infuses splashes of colour with vibrant patterns that unleash energy for the viewer. Upon seeing his work, many visitors to the gallery say they found hope, happiness and energy in his art.

David Zinger is an employee engagement expert from Winnipeg, Canada. The origin of People Artistry can be traced to a conversation between Peter and David. David had watched Peter painting. He also observed Peter's caring, enthusiasm and ability to bring out the best in the people who worked at Rideau. David said to Peter, "You are an artist and your paintings are enthralling but you are also a People Artist. Your workplace is your studio, people are your medium and your canvas is filled with recognition, connection and engagement."

Rosa Say, a management expert from Hawaii, said the challenge of the book was, "how to teach somebody else 'to be a Hart' or how do you enable someone else to be a People Artist?"

This book is our response to her question. You don't need to become Peter Hart - we encourage and enable you to create your own People Artistry to bring out the best in others.

An Introduction to People Artistry

Imagine a workplace where people don't care. Imagine spending eight hours a day working in anonymity. Imagine being told that the only recognition you need is your salary. We hope you would only have to imagine this, not experience it.

There is another way, People Artistry.

**People Artists
draw out the best in
themselves and others
to create a workplace
canvas of excellence
for the benefit
of all.**

Here are six primers from the People Artists we interviewed.

Don Macpherson is the president of Modern Survey in Minneapolis, Minnesota. Every Thanksgiving Day, Don drives to his office, rather than parking himself on his sofa to watch the annual Thursday afternoon NFL football match. He phones upwards of 120 employees, friends, family members, associates, and customers to individually thank them for the previous 12 months. Don literally puts abundant thanks into Thanksgiving.

Henry Mintzberg, a professor at McGill University in Montreal and one of the world's leading management writers and educators, believes that management is an art, craft and science. Henry offers a no nonsense approach to management, leadership and strategy. Dismissing the distinction between leaders and managers, he simply declares that good managers lead and good leaders manage. He describes engaging managers as those who demonstrate respect, trust, caring, inspiration and listening to bring out the "energy that exists naturally within people." "You don't learn to manage by completing an MBA," added Mintzberg.

Rosa Say, a management educator and coach from Hawaii, wrote *Managing with Aloha*. She teaches managers to practice the Daily Five Minutes or D5M. Managers offer five minutes of their time to fully listen to the people who work with them. The staff set the agenda for the conversation. Often skeptical at first, the majority of managers say it is one of the best things they ever did at work and many take the Daily Five Minutes home and practice it with their spouse and children.

Larissa Thurlow and Kelly Saretsky work together in Institutional Research and Planning at the College of North Atlantic in Doha, Qatar. They maintain that each is the other's People Artist because of their mutual caring, playfulness and how they feed off each other's ideas. It is not unusual to hear them say at the same moment, "We are saying the same thing, only differently." They embrace their differences to achieve results that neither of them could achieve alone.

Srikant Chellappa, based in St. Louis, Missouri and the co-founder of Engagedly, has worked with up to 1,200 people in an IT firm. He is also an independent film producer working with 40 to 60 people on a set. Whether in front of a computer or behind a camera, Srikant believes we must connect people to their aspirations. Srikant attributes his success to being perceptive about the people he works with, while wedding their aspirations to the organization or project goal.

The People Artists we interviewed for this book told us how important it is to bring out the best in others. They practiced their art in different ways but were united in their caring, listening, action-orientation, and strong drive to create meaningful results. They told us how important it was to carve out space and time to draw out the best in others.

People Artists: Drawing Out the Best in Others at Work is our second People Artistry book. The first book, *People Artistry at Work: The Ennoblement Imperative*, set the stage for People Artistry. Our second book offers you: stories and insights from thirty-seven People Artists, practices to work on at the end of each chapter, five tools relating to heart, head and hands, and a self-assessment of your own People Artistry.

Michael Stallard, author of *Connection Culture*, has demonstrated how important it is for People Artists to have their finger on the pulse of both the organization and the individual by using vision, value and voice to guide and drive action. Kym Fawcett, Manager of Safety and Social Responsibility in Calgary, Alberta, maintains that People Artists sketch out the greater picture, bring people together to foster creative ideas and ensure a finished body of work that fits with everyone's vision.

To bring out the best in others, People Artists also ensure they bring out the best in themselves. Lisa Sansome, working in Ontario, Canada, said People Artistry is, "about knowing yourself, knowing your strengths, and learning how to know others and their strengths too. It's about being positive-oriented and future-directed. It's about constructive criticism and growth mindsets. It's about having the best interests of others at heart, all the time, and realizing that there are always trade-offs."

Will you embark with us on this interpersonal journey? You will be challenged to drop your own agenda and maybe, even your ego. You will be asked to be attentive with others. You will refuse to let opportunities to recognize and appreciate others slip away, despite the one hundred and one demands on your time. You will offer your energy and your words to make someone's day, and to do that every day.

If you engage with the challenge of People Artistry, you might discover what Don MacPherson said about his annual eight-hour Thanksgiving Day gratitude ritual. It would be so easy to just stay home and watch the game, "but I do it because I really appreciate the contributions so many people have made in my work and family life. But in all honesty, I think I might be the one who gets the most from it."

Henry Mintzberg stated the best management book in his course is an empty book given to participants to record their insights. We believe the same about People Artistry. We encourage you to work with an empty notebook or computer document to keep track of your progress with the recommended practices.

Your Practice

Artists engage with their work. To be a People Artist, you must go beyond reading and engage with what you read. Each chapter offers you two exercises to practice.

1. Who are the People Artists in your life? Who brought out the best in you at work or home? Write about how they did this and how you can incorporate this into your own People Artistry.

2. A number of brief anecdotes were used to start this chapter. What stories or experiences in your work or workplace stand out as good examples of People Artistry? What can you learn from those stories?

Painting at right: "Red Haven"

CHAPTER 2

People Artistry is Good Business

You know how important achieving results are for business. But what about building relationships? What happens when you fail to acknowledge others, to help them grow, to engage with them so that they will engage with their work?

People Artistry is not only good for others and good for you - People Artistry is good business. Yet our workplaces are often challenged and frayed; challenged by the volume of things requiring our attention and frayed with disengagement. We feel squeezed with too much to do and scattered by the sheer range of things demanding our attention. With our smartphones, tablets and laptops, we can work from anywhere and the boundaries between work and home have vanished. Many of us roll out of bed in the morning and before we brush our teeth we check our phone for email and texts from work.

During an environmental conference in Tucson, Arizona, a participant from a Fortune 500 company said it best, "We have gone from doing more with less, to doing everything with nothing." We can get so caught up in the demands of our work that we feel we have nothing left for the people at work.

On April 9, 2015, Gallup declared that employee engagement levels in the United States had decreased to 31.7%. Since 2012, engagement rates have never been above 38%. Woven into Gallup's assessment of engagement are many elements of People Artistry: best work, caring, recognition, praise, strengths, encouragement, friendship, conversation, learning and growth. When these elements are alive in the workplace engagement rates are high, as are financial success, productivity, profitability, customer satisfaction and well-being.

David MacLeod and Nita Clarke received the Order of the British Empire for their work on employee engagement. The UK's Engage for Success movement found four lenses or enablers for engagement: strategic narrative, good managers, employee voice, and ethical integrity. During the interview for this book, MacLeod said that the approach to improving engagement and People Artistry were similar: "We diminish people by ignoring them - bringing authentic employee voice into the organization is the cheapest smoke alarm you will ever have for organizational disengagement."

The Engage for Success movement, sponsored by the UK government, compiled the business evidence for engagement. Employee engagement contributes to: income, growth, safety, customer satisfaction, profits, performance, productivity, innovation, retention and well-being. The evidence was gathered from individual organizations, research consultancies and academia. The business case for engagement was so solid that the document was aptly titled, "Nailing the Evidence".

Our brain is challenged to work on results while also building relationships. David Rock, co-founder of the NeuroLeadership Institute, frequently refers to a study of 60,000 leaders and managers conducted by the Management Research Group which found that only 0.77% of those surveyed were perceived as being strong when delivering on both results and relationships. This represents only 462 People Artists out of 60,000 managers!

Rock referred to this as the "brain's neural seesaw" because the results section of the brain interferes with the relationship section, and vice versa. If the collective leadership group was sitting on a teeter-totter, we would find leaders cementing the results section to the ground while relationships would be up in the air. This is why there is such a need for People Artists; without developing solid relationships, business results easily become stuck or grounded.

We want you to achieve results and build relationships. We want you to make a difference for yourself, your organization, and your staff. We don't want you to abandon science, numbers and results. And as you work on People Artistry, you will find that People Artistry will begin to work on you.

Your Practice

1. Be mindful of your neural seesaw for the next seven days. Notice which domains, results or relationships, are easier for you to work with. Pay attention to what it takes to switch from one focus to the other. Are you able to achieve results for your area while building relationships with your team?

2. Scan your business and yourself. Are you energized or depleted? Are you more likely to look at one of your screens than the person in front of you? Is there space in your day for meaningful connection with others? Determine how much time you can devote each day to practicing People Artistry. A realistic 3-minute commitment is better than a 15-minute vague intention.

CHAPTER 3

An Invitation to People Artistry

When you read the book title what was on your mind? Did you think we were going to ask you to work with paint and crayons, or make you post a picture on the office fridge? Did you think this was going to be a fluffy soft-skills book to be tossed because of all the "real" work you must do? Do you believe that the human element of work is covered with the platitude: *people are our greatest resource*?

Imagine what it must be like to work in a job you hate. Or worse, imagine being stuck in an unwanted career - unable to leave because you lack the skills for another profession and need the money to make ends meet. Each new day would be filled with dread as you get into your car, driving to the office/prison where you'll serve that day's portion of your sentence.

We know from history and our own experiences that work tends to be like a relationship. Good ones lift us. Bad ones depress us. In each case, the relationship probably consumes about one-third of our daily lives. We'll either spend that time living with the burden of dealing with a toxic workplace and unsatisfying work or digging into stimulating projects with friends.

Joop de Kler, from Amsterdam said that People Artistry invites us to realize that "every encounter offers the chance of a new creation."

Are you a People Artist?

Of course you know the answer to this question is not a simple yes or no. For example, everyone can draw, but some of us can draw much better than others. We believe that People Artistry, much like drawing, can be learned through example, instruction and practice. And we want you to learn how to be better at drawing out the best in others.

Let's take a snapshot of where you are now. Below is an informal self-assessment. Don't make too much out of it as we consider it a nudge, not a diagnosis.

Answer each statement with a yes or no. Put a check mark beside the statements that you agree with.

☐ 1.   I am able to draw out my personal best at work every day.

☐ 2.   I give more to others than I expect to receive.

☐ 3.   I see people as people — not human resources.

☐ 4.   I am authentic and transparent in how I work.

☐ 5.   I recognize at least one person every day at work.

☐ 6.   I listen more than I talk.

☐ 7.   I am energized when I recognize and engage others.

☐ 8.   I am genuinely curious about people.

☐ 9.   I am willing and able to invest energy and time into developing others.

☐ 10. I believe results and relationships are not mutually exclusive.

☐ 11. I am equally comfortable achieving results and building relationships.

☐ 12. I offer my full attention to the person in front of me.

☐ 13. I offer others specific and detailed feedback.

☐ 14. I support the well-being of others at work.

☐ 15. I can listen without judging or giving immediate advice.

☐ 16. I offer frequent caring and constructive feedback.

☐ 17. I look forward to working with people at work every day.

□   18.   I am aware of what motivates others.

□   19.   I frequently talk about the meaning of work and how people matter.

□   20.   I am attuned to the uniqueness and individuality of people.

□   21.   I believe focusing on people is a pathway to sustainable results.

□   22.   I am competent with my interpersonal skills.

□   23.   I feel rewarded at the end of the day for how I worked with others.

□   24.   I am comfortable working with emotions, energy, and engagement.

□   25.   I demonstrate robust caring for people at work every day.

Total the number of check marks to calculate your score

Score _____ out of 25.

The more check marks the stronger your artistry.

- If you scored 24 or 25, you can use this book to tweak and support your artistry and you might share this book with another budding People Artist.

- If you scored 20 to 23, you are doing very well and this book should confirm you are on the right path while offering you fresh perspectives or practices.

- If you scored 15 to 19, you are showing potential as a People Artist and can build from this foundation to enhance your artistry.

- A score of 14 or less is a trigger for you to study this book and commit to doing the exercises to develop your comfort and competence with People Artistry.

People Artists realize three immediate and potentially lasting benefits from their work:

- You will have more allies and engaged co-workers. No one wants to team up with a nasty co-worker. By contrast, People Artists who observe and publicly recognize good work, tend to attract collaborators.

- More collaborators and willing allies mean more resources; which, in turn, gets more done.

- You will have a higher level of well-being derived from positive emotions, engagement, relationships, meaning, achievement and strengths.

Your Practice

1. If you have not already done so, complete the short People Artistry self-assessment. Look for strengths and identify areas that you can strengthen. Commit to working on People Artistry for the next three weeks. Complete the assessment again after three weeks to determine if you have improved. You could also ask someone who knows you well to complete the questionnaire as if they were you. Do your two scores match? Use the results as a trigger for a dialogue with the other person and don't get defensive about their assessment. Instead thank them for the feedback, even if you see some items differently.

2. Identify an outcome at work that is significant to you. Perhaps it is a decrease in accidents, an increase in sales, or a boost to the next employee engagement score. Apply your practice of People Artistry to those results and determine if working on People Artistry for six weeks not only develops your artistry skills but also contributes to your desired outcome.

CHAPTER 4

The People Artistry Palette

Our interviews with the People Artists demonstrated a diversity of tools and approaches. Phil Gebyshak makes exceptional use of social media tools to connect and grow people. Warren Heppner applies his rehabilitation knowledge to bring out the best in people even after devastating work-related injuries. Philip Dundas uses food to nourish people in Northern Ireland prisons. Leslee Thompson fuses caring, connection and People Artistry into her role as President and CEO of Kingston General Hospital in Ontario.

Although each artist may work with a wide variety of people tools, we offer you a basic palette of People Artistry. Think of it as a starting point and reference point when you return to work on the fundamentals.

At the core of the People Artistry Palette is the purpose of the tools – to draw out the best in others. The first ring around the core is based on five parts of the body: heart, ears, eyes, lips and hand. We are using parts of the body to represent how fundamental People Artistry is and stress that People Artistry is never any further away from you than your heart, head and hands.

The second ring from the center of the Palette indicates the function of each of the tools:

1. The heart cares.
2. The ears listen.
3. The eyes see.
4. The lips talk.
5. The hands give.

What glues the second ring together is conversation. You cannot be a People Artist without fully engaging with others. Conversation is a pathway that requires caring, listening, seeing, talking and giving. For example, what initially began as interviews with our People Artists rapidly became engaging conversations.

Vincent Miholic, an Organization Learning and Development Specialist for the State of Louisiana, said, "Artistry is an on-going process – sometimes successful, sometimes not – which requires risk-taking, initiative, perseverance, acquired practices, absence from distraction, flow and a sense of excellence."

The outer ring of the People Artistry Palette is based on five domains used by Rideau's Vistance Learning – an online management development program for getting recognition right. The five scientifically validated domains are: Praiseworthy Actions, Acknowledging Intent, Recognition Talking, Appreciative Listening and Rewarding Giving.

The Vistance Learning platform focuses on the importance and impact of recognition to influence performance and engagement. It guides managers through a prescribed set of brief, yet significant, learning modules based on their individual assessment. At the end of each of the next five chapters, we will offer specific tips from Vistance Learning to enhance your development.

When Peter starts a painting he looks at the blank canvas and imagines that the painting will be the very best he has ever done. It is a positive and energizing experience. It may not be the best, but he learns from the experience and applies this to his next painting. Every painting reflects the sum total of all the previous paintings Peter has created. Likewise, People Artistry is something you will get better at with experience.

Your Practice

1. Based on what you have read so far, initiate conversations with others at work about People Artistry. How would they define it? When have they experienced someone else's People Artistry? What do they see helping or hindering People Artistry within your organization?

2. Either develop a five-day plan to focus on one of the elements of People Artistry each day or a five-week plan to focus on one of the People Artistry elements each week. Use the next five chapters to kick-start your work and see how you can create artistry with your heart, head and hands.

CHAPTER 5

Care: The Heart of the People Artist

You know when someone cares. You can tell almost immediately, perhaps without even being able to articulate it. Of course, that also means other people know when you care. Without genuine caring, work becomes careless — while apathy, inertia and disengagement take root in our relationships, teams, departments and company.

Without the heart of caring, People Artistry has form but no substance. Caring can be challenging. You need discipline, concentration and patience. Caring requires trust and transparency.

Richard Carreiro was David's professor and thesis advisor in the Faculty of Education at the University of Manitoba in Winnipeg, Canada. Richard expressed his caring simply, "I've learned to take people as they come, more than what I necessarily want them to be. It all begins with acceptance."

Kevin Sheridan, an expert on employee engagement, shared an inspiring encounter with a People Artist in the climbing world, Vern Tejas. Kevin loves to climb and has summited four of the world's top seven peaks.

On one occasion, Kevin was preparing to climb Mount Elbrus in Russia. Before ascending the mountain, Vern, the guide for this expedition and a very experienced climber, held a team meeting during which Kevin admitted in front of the entire team that he was afraid of the steep vertical sections of the climb. Vern acknowledged Kevin's courage in publicly admitting to his fear and told him, "Don't worry, I've got your back."

During the challenging section of the climb, Vern was never too far away. He did not say anything but in the most reassuring of gestures, gently touched Kevin's elbow twice during this section of the ascent.

Sometimes a simple gesture from a People Artist is all we need to reach the summit – whether that summit is a mountain or a large organizational objective.

Emma McClees, the Safety Manager for the city of Chula Vista in California, responded to a question about what makes a People Artist, "They contribute enough to leave a lasting mark and spark the thought, 'I am better today because I have known you'." We are certain Kevin Sheridan would say that about Vern Tejas!

Dick Richards wrote *Artful Work: Awakening Joy, Meaning, and Commitment in the Workplace.* He believes the reward for artful work is in the doing, artful work requires consistent and conscious use of the self and as the artist creates the work, the work creates the artist. Yet many of us are uncomfortable with emotions and energy in the workplace and this holds us back from being more artistic in our work. Richards declared, "a successful leader is adept at dealing with emotion." Brady Wilson, the co-founder of Juice Inc. concurs, "Energy resides in tension and we derive tremendous energy for work by working with tension rather than avoiding it."

Leslee Thompson, the President and CEO of Kingston General Hospital in Ontario, Canada, told us how caring helped both her and the hospital move through a major patient challenge and in the process become a leading hospital for patient engagement. Caring begins with self-care, bringing out the best in you. Leslee said something remarkable about People Artistry. Talking about leading a large hospital, she said, "Something happens when you are comfortable in your own skin. You no longer need a thick skin - you become a permeable membrane and your leadership and People Artistry flows through you and out of you to those you lead."

A good heart goes a long way when it comes to forging relationships. We create safety in relationships and teams when others know we care about them and care about what they are trying to achieve. This also gives us a strong foundation to confront them on gaps in performance or resolving conflicts.

A central tip from the Praiseworthy Action section of Rideau's Vistance Learning Platform is to ensure you take time to find out what is meaningful to those you work with and to demonstrate authentic and genuine caring for those around you. Keep that in mind as you tackle this chapter's exercises.

Your Practice

1. As you work on various goals (summits) at work, demonstrate caring for everyone you are working with. Help them to express their fears while also letting them know "you've got their back." Determine what gestures you can express to help others move through the tricky parts of a project or process.

2. Take the word CARE and make an acronym out of the 4 letters as a guide for your gestures of caring. For example CARE could be Compassion-Acceptance-Recognition-Enthusiasm or CARE could be Create-Acknowledge-Respect-Engage. Use the acronym CARE as a trigger to show you care and demonstrate that caring is also an action, not just an emotion.

CHAPTER 6

Listen: The Ears of the Artist

You can't read a management or leadership book without the author talking about the importance of listening. You know that listening is more than nodding your head and saying "go on" as the other person talks. Take time to fully listen and ensure you pour your energy into understanding the people you work with.

Marshall Goldsmith concludes his presentations and emails with the line, "Life is good". We asked him: "Given your breadth and depth of experience, what are the two best ways a manager or leader can bring out the best in people?"

Here was his reply:

1. *Managers can ask for input from their staff on how they (the managers) can become more effective.*

2. *Managers can then listen, ask about this input and follow-up with their staff to ensure effective implementation.*

When we ask, listen, act and follow up at work, we can supplement "Life is good" with "Work is good."

Jasmine Gartner works in London as an anthropologist focused on organizations and engagement. She recently wrote an insightful book on work, *Employee Engagement: A Little Book of Big Ideas.* She defined a People Artist as "someone who has vision. But also, it's someone who can tune into their environment and really listen, not just to the words (though of course those are important), but to know when to push a bit, to dig a little deeper."

Celestine McMullen Allen experienced a tough challenge in a training course while she was attempting to roll out a new performance management initiative. The participants had a lack of

31   *Painting at left: "Maïa 1"*

trust and a high degree of skepticism surrounding the entire initiative. She sensed it in the room and rather than ignoring it or ploughing through the material, she stopped training to fully listen to what the participants had to say and how they were feeling. She cared about the participants' views while also challenging them about the change that was occurring. Celeste said she was rewarded for her caring by their involvement during the remainder of the training and especially remembers one participant who came up to her at the end and said, "You became real to us."

Gail Pischak, founder of Shared Visions in Regina, Saskatchewan, told us about holding a space for others to enter. We invite people to enter the space with acceptance and curiosity. Questions are a powerful way to draw out the best in others.

Questions are making a comeback. A critic of education back in the 1970's, Neil Postman lamented, "Children enter school as question marks and leave as periods." Warren Berger, in 2014, wrote *A More Beautiful Question: The Power of Inquiry to Spark Breakthrough Ideas*. A beautiful question is an ambitious, yet actionable, question that can shift the way we think and act as a catalyst for change.

Warren told us:

> *Questions tend to be more engaging than statements. A statement is closed off; one either agrees with it or not. A question is more open and inviting and full of possibilities. So if an organization poses big ambitious questions and invites people to try to help answer them (How might we do a better job at X?), it becomes a good tool for engaging people and tapping into their imaginations and problem-solving skills. And often, the more ambitious the question is, the more it will challenge people and really get them thinking and exploring. For this reason, I've suggested that companies might, in some cases, actually be better off using "mission questions" in place of mission statements.*

A vital tip in the Appreciative Listening section of Rideau's Vistance Learning Platform is to remove distractions that interfere with listening while fully tuning into the meaning behind an employee's words and tone of voice. Keep that in mind as you tackle this chapter's exercises.

Your Practice

1. Marshall Goldsmith is probably the best known leadership coach in the world. He just gave you some advice that some leaders and companies have paid millions of dollars to receive. Ask your staff how you can become more effective. Listen fully to what they say. Ask questions for clarification. Take action. Follow up with your staff to ensure effective implementation.

2. Pose a beautiful question to bring out the best in the people you work with. Remember it should be ambitious and actionable. Perhaps the question is: What can we do together so that work is better for our organization, our clients and ourselves? Maybe the question is more basic: What is the beautiful question we need to ask ourselves every day to achieve results while building relationships?

CHAPTER 7

See: The Eyes of the Artist

Do you see what is going on around you at work? Do you notice when someone cut their hair or wears a new outfit? Do you see when someone is struggling? Do you see the contributions being made at work? Do you have vision for what is possible?

In many museums around the world, people are turning their backs to masterpieces, pulling out their phone or camera and taking a selfie with the work of art. On one hand, it is nice to be in the same frame as the art; yet on the other hand, people are failing to see firsthand what is right in front of them. A People Artist may take a selfie with the people she works with, but she will also see the person directly in front of her.

Ira M. Ozer, from Chappaqua, New York, told us about Randy Gilson from Pittsburgh who bought a dilapidated building and made the building come alive with art. Gilson saw potential, where others saw an eyesore. The building is now open to the public. Ozer believes Gilson used a physical structure to model and bring out the best in others by demonstrating that anything is possible with vision and collaboration.

Steve Roesler, a leading management consultant, offers clients practical ways to be extraordinary. He is also a loving husband who has supported his wife through a very difficult medical journey throughout the past two years. Steve's People Artistry at work is powerful, yet pales in comparison to his devotion to his wife. He was eager to give his time to talk about People Artistry and said, "People Artists start with a clean brush."

We must begin with a clear set of eyes and eliminate preconceived notions about people. According to Steve, People Artists make people feel, not just see. He said that the organization is the canvas and people are the colours. People Artists "help individuals paint a portrait that clearly reflects exactly who they are; so that if they were a portrait in a gallery, anyone walking past would have a clear picture as well."

Michael O'Malley, Vice President and National Practice Leader of Higher Education at Sibson Consulting, co-wrote *Every Leader is an Artist*. It is a wonderful adjunct book to the People Artistry books. From the book jacket:

> *Artists put their work on display for everyone to judge, accepting a position of vulnerability for want of something important to say and in the service of contributing to the common good. Artists bring people closer together by providing a forum for shared experiences. Artists challenge, excite, comfort, and motivate people, and they don't learn their craft by reading about it in a book; they practice, push themselves and their means of expression and execute, execute, execute. These are exactly the same things effective business leaders do day in and day out.*

When your eyes are open to the best in others, you just might be amazed at what you see. And what you see will be people and sustainable results achieved through the artistry of achieving those results, while simultaneously building relationships.

A key tip in the Acknowledging Intent section of Rideau's Vistance Learning Platform is to value and respect people while also recognizing the impact recognition has on both engagement and performance. Keep that in mind as you tackle this chapter's exercises.

Your Practice

1. Are you putting your People Artistry on display? Do you let people know how much you care with words and actions? Tomorrow at work, take time to stop, notice and comment to five people about what you see or how you have seen them change.

2. Craft your vision for People Artistry. How will you and the people you work with be better because of People Artistry? Perhaps you could start with a beautiful question about what people would see and hear from you that would let them know you care about them and want to bring out their best.

Painting at right: "Once"

CHAPTER 8

Talk: The Lips of the Artist

You can express with gestures and with words. Never overlook the power of an expression of gratitude to make someone's day or maybe, even his or her month or year. How many times have you failed to speak up about someone's contribution or effort?

Amanda Page, a Change Lead for Cisco in the UK, told us about the power of a few words.

> *There was a lot of change in our organization and we had invested a lot of time, effort, and passion in an organization that was no longer going to be in place. It was hard to let go. Our manager instructed us to put together a list of the elements of our role we will stop, start, continue and defer or handover.*

> *It was a good exercise, but I was still struggling to let go. Going through this process made me feel sad that we were no longer able to continue. As a Change Lead, I understand the challenges of letting go so it was interesting for me to notice how I was managing myself through this process.*

> *We were asked to set up a meeting with two leaders who might be interested in some of our work. We were to make a presentation for them to decide what they would like. "Oh my," I thought "this just gets worse. It's like a Yard Sale!" The leaders looked through the content and focused on different elements and asked lots of questions and were genuinely interested. I started to feel better.*

> *Suddenly, one of the leaders said "What you have created here is fantastic! Be confident and know that all the good work you have done and your legacy will live on and be of real value to me and others."*

> *It was like a fog had lifted and I was ready to move on. Now that is People Artistry - acknowledgement and appreciation from an intuitive leader. I love this story and I tell*

it all the time with leaders and employees as we can get bogged down in the task and forget about people.

Sue Mitten, an Organizational Development Consultant at the University of Regina, has also experienced the power of words. "I was the recipient of People Artistry. It wasn't prompted as it was in a coffee line. The person just said, 'You do good work.' That's all. One statement and I buoyed my entire day and I remember it six months later!"

Doug Shaw, an expert on work and engagement in the UK, stated: "I think developing the habit of awareness and presence helps make someone a People Artist. A willingness to suspend judgement when new ideas are forming helps too; as does being kind. Never underestimate the artistic power of simple things."

Peter Dyck, a retired management consultant, has been sharing lunches with David for 20 years. Although they are both nourished by the food, it is Peter's words of encouragement that have nourished David over the past two decades. Do you take time to meet with your colleagues?

A central tip in the Recognition Talking section in Rideau's Vistance Learning Platform is to ensure that your feedback is specific and that you let people know how their actions made a difference to you, their peers, a customer or to the company. Keep that in mind as you tackle this chapter's exercises.

Your Practice

1. Ask yourself: Who have I failed to acknowledge, recognize, or appreciate today? Your answer to that question has two parts. Part one is to generate a list of names. Part two is to connect with the people on your list and offer verbal or written acknowledgement.

2. Take a few extra moments before you recognize someone to ensure your recognition is specific. Although even general feedback or recognition can have an impact, specific feedback lets the other person know that you are attentive.

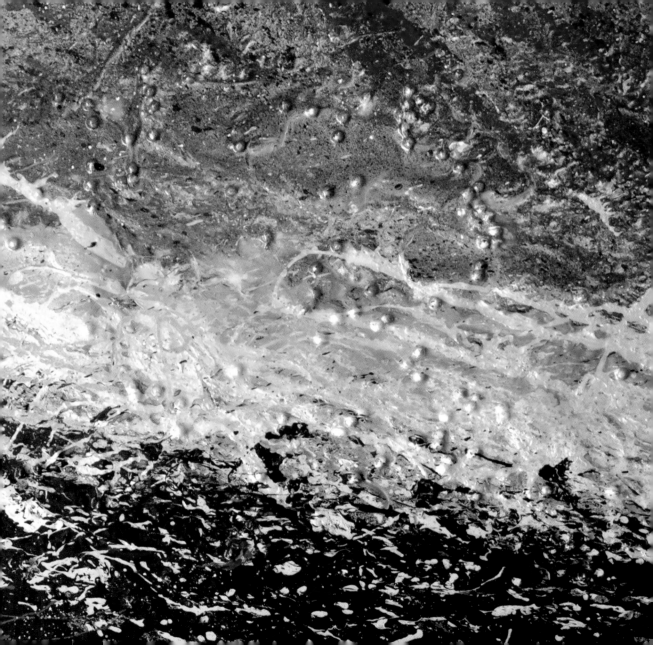

CHAPTER 9

Give: The Hands of the People Artist

Art is giving. Whether it's through a publically displayed painting or an act of kindness to a co-worker, all artistry requires is that you give of yourself. What are you giving at work? How much of yourself do you give to your work? You don't want to lose yourself in your work as that can result in burnout but also be careful of holding back. If you keep holding back at work, you might not burnout - you might rustout.

Richard Carreiro, when asked to define People Artistry, gave us the gift of a short poem by Rachel Field that he believed said it better than he could.

Some People

Isn't it strange some people make

You feel so tired inside

Your thoughts begin to shrivel up

Like leaves all brown and dried!

But when you're with some other ones,

It's stranger still to find

Your thoughts as thick as fireflies

All shiny in your mind!

People Artists give to their world. They put themselves into their work through expressions and interactions. Early in his career, David worked as a Youth Care Worker in Winnipeg with fourteen juvenile boys living in a residential treatment centre. The work was hard, but it was David's relationship with Dushyanta Persaud, a co-worker and People Artist, that helped David survive the volatile atmosphere of that work. Dushyanta became a Superintendent in the Winnipeg School Division. His authentic support, playful presence and optimistic outlook were his People Artistry tools to bring out the best in students, teachers and staff.

Dnyan Shah works in Pune, India. She is the Senior Vice President and Global Head of Employee Engagement for Mphasis, a $930 million dollar IT company with over 48,000 employees. When asked about People Artistry, she said:

> People Artists have vision and are in the know of what needs to be created. Team members are moving colours that fill up the canvas. The artist's role is to guide them continuously towards the eventual creation.

Dnyan said, "The artist is always the enabler and the team is the achiever." When asked for examples of her artistry at work, Dnyan elaborated:

> I had a team of leaders (remote) who communicated with each other only through emails. They had built walls around themselves and were guarding their own territories. I started doing daily calls with them, initially everyone found the calls to be unnecessary but soon enough they realized the worth of resolving issues over calls and the emails stopped and their response times become much faster.

The true assessment and value of People Artistry is demonstrated in how your artistry is received. Dnyan sent us some feedback that she received from her team. Here are short excerpts from two team members:

> There is no doubt of how much she genuinely cares for the team. Whether it's early in the morning, or late at night, she is there for us. She makes us feel valued, special, and important.

> Dnyan makes me feel good about work and myself. She has a power to transform my challenges into strengths every day. She has never said "no" to a new idea. I attribute my good work to her understanding, openness and perceptiveness.

Kevin Sheridan, the CEO climber we met in Chapter 5, was concerned about the amount of work he was asking of his staff at one of his former companies. They knew he cared about them. So when he approached Ashleigh, a key employee in the organization, and voiced his concern about the spike in workload, she responded with understanding. She knew the work and the results were important to Kevin and the company, reassuring him by saying, "Don't worry, I grew up on a farm and when it is harvest time, it is harvest time."

When People Artists invest in others, they report how frequently people invest in them and in the results they are trying to achieve.

A key distinction made in the Rewarding Giving section in Rideau's Vistance Learning Platform is to know the difference between reward and recognition and to ensure that when you give tangible recognition it is accompanied by spoken or written words of appreciation. Keep that in mind as you tackle this chapter's exercises.

Your Practice

1. Determine the ways you give of yourself at work and be determined to give even more of yourself. As you give more of yourself, notice what happens to your overall energy for work and watch what happens to the people you work with. Document the changes.

2. Find something tangible you can give when you offer someone a statement of appreciation or gratitude. We have seen someone treasure a packet of sugar, a penny, or even a small blank piece of torn paper when it was paired with a sincere compliment. Giving something tangible makes caring powerful. The other person sees the item as symbolizing your care and their worth in your eyes. Even a very 'insignificant' item becomes significant when it is paired with care.

CHAPTER 10

Sustainable People Artistry

We trust you have found value, insight, inspiration and guidance in this journey through People Artistry. David defines employee engagement in eight words: good work done well with others every day. A People Artist performs good work, does it well, knows how much others play a key role in all work and does it every day. Good work is sustainable and People Artistry is a powerful pathway to employee engagement.

We encourage you to learn and grow by using People Artistry to improve others, organizations and yourself. The thirty-seven people we interviewed were unanimous in not being complacent or thinking that they had arrived as People Artists. People Artistry is a daily endeavour, perhaps even a calling. In the words of Vincent Miholic, "Satisfaction is an example of complacency; engagement is an example of artistry."

Philip Dundas founded The Kitchen Table Project, a social enterprise project focusing on the ways that cooking can support people in need. He has worked with the Northern Ireland Prison Service using his People Artistry with cooking to help young offenders.

Just as Philip nourishes people in need with his culinary artistry, we trust you were interpersonally nourished through the stories, statements, images and practices of this book. But you've also just begun; People Artistry is a lifetime journey. We know this because of the Harvard Grant Study that followed 268 men for 75 years. Dr. George Vailliant, who led the study for many years, found that solid interpersonal relationships were the best predictor of long-term well-being. With 75 years of research to substantiate his claim, Vailliant declared, "The most important finding proves that the only thing that really matters in life, are your relationships to other people."

We started this book with anecdotes from six of the thirty-seven People Artists we interviewed. Let's conclude with a statement from Maria Soledad Ristra, working in Paris, who offered this perspective on artistry:

I believe, as many others, that we are all artists of life. We all possess the beauty, the richness, the creativity and the potential to show up colourfully, brightly and uniquely. Our unique, genuine voice, that speaks the truth about who we really are, is our artist's bag; it's the brush with which we paint the world we want for us and our loved ones, the pen with which we write the words we choose to communicate and the realities we create through them, the instrument we play bringing harmony or disruptive sounds to our lives, the music we sing through what we say and how we say it. Our art is, therefore, the way we show up in the world.

Your Practice

1. As with any art form, People Artistry takes practice to master. We encourage you to return often to this book to hone your skills by revisiting the practices aligned with Rideau's research-backed Vistance Learning Platform. Visit www.VistanceLearning.com to experience a free trial and learn additional ways to add colour to your People Artistry Palette. To learn more, you can also contact Jennifer Lumba at Vistance Learning: JenniferLumba@Rideau.com

2. We trust you will keep exploring People Artistry at work. Your final challenge is to make your practice a daily discipline. We encourage you to journey on this path and believe that seeing a number of the recipients of your People Artistry also become People Artists will enrich and sustain you in your art.

Painting at right: "Hurricane of Colors 2"

Peter W. Hart
CEO Rideau Recognition Solutions

Peter has been one of the driving forces in transforming Rideau into one of the world's fastest growing Reward and Recognition providers. He was recognized as an Ernst & Young 2008 Entrepreneur of the Year Finalist. Peter served on Recognition Professionals International Board of Directors from 2004 to 2010 and was recently re-elected to that Board. He was the founder of the Recognition Council, a Strategic Industry Group within the Incentive Marketing Association, which helps provide recognition best practice guidance to the industry. In 2009, he was elected to the Board of Directors of the Incentive Federation, the umbrella organization for the entire incentive and recognition industry. Peter also serves on the Board of Directors of Accueil Bonneau, the oldest homeless shelter in Montreal. Peter is very active in social media through his blog, Twitter, and Facebook pages. He is regarded as an industry expert who has authored numerous articles and speaks at industry events. Peter is married and has a handful of children, and more than a handful of grandchildren who are always looking for recognition and rewards! Peter also paints. You can visit his gallery in Old Montreal and see his latest collections online at www. PETERwHART.com.

David Zinger
David Zinger & Associates

David Zinger is an employee engagement speaker and consultant. He has devoted over 14,000 hours to the topic, in addition to founding and hosting the 6,700 member Employee Engagement Network. David has written four books on work, a dozen e-books and over 2,500 blog posts on employee engagement. David developed a 10-block pyramid of engagement to focus on results, performance, progress, relationships, recognition, moments, strengths, meaning, well-being and energy. He uses small, simple, strategic and sustainable actions to improve engagement, results and relationships. David has worked on engagement in Singapore, Wales, Qatar, England, South Africa, Germany, Spain, Poland, UAE, United States and Canada. David is married to Susan and they have three children. To learn more about David visit: www.davidzinger.com.

Acknowledgements

This book exists because of the input and voices of the thirty-seven People Artists who contributed their thoughts, experiences, perspectives and stories. Their unique perspectives and collective voice for People Artistry helped craft a deeper, richer and human tapestry for this book.

Our admiration and gratitude to: Celestine McMullen Allen, Warren Berger, Denise Bissonnette, Richard Carreiro, Srikant Chellappa, Philip Dundas, Peter Dyck, Kym Fawcett, Jasmine Gartner, Phil Gerbyshak, Marshall Goldsmith, Warren Heppner, Joop de Kler, Isabelle Lavigne, David MacLeod, Emma McClees, Don McPherson, Vincent Miholic, Henry Mintzberg, Sue Mitten, Michael O'Malley, Ira Ozer, Amanda Page, Dushyanta Persaud, Gail Pischak, Manon Provencher, Dick Richards, Lisa Sansome, Kelly Saretsky, Dnyan Shah, Kevin Sheridan, Maria Soledad Ristra, Steve Roesler, Rosa Say, Doug Shaw, Michael Stallard, Leslee Thompson, Larissa Thurlow and Brady Wilson.

In addition to the thirty-seven people we interviewed for this work, a book does not exist without contributions from many people. We are especially grateful for the contributions of: Armelle Rapin, Francine Bellomo, Tim Beyers, Susan Gerlach, Gordon Green, Nancy Guitard, Jordan Hart, Lisa Legault, Jennifer Lumba, Tom Miller, John Mills, Andrea O'Neill, Roy Saunderson, Charles Scherbaum, Valerie Shaw, Kiki Stefanakis, Isabelle Lavigne and Manon Provencher.

Painting at right: "Ray"

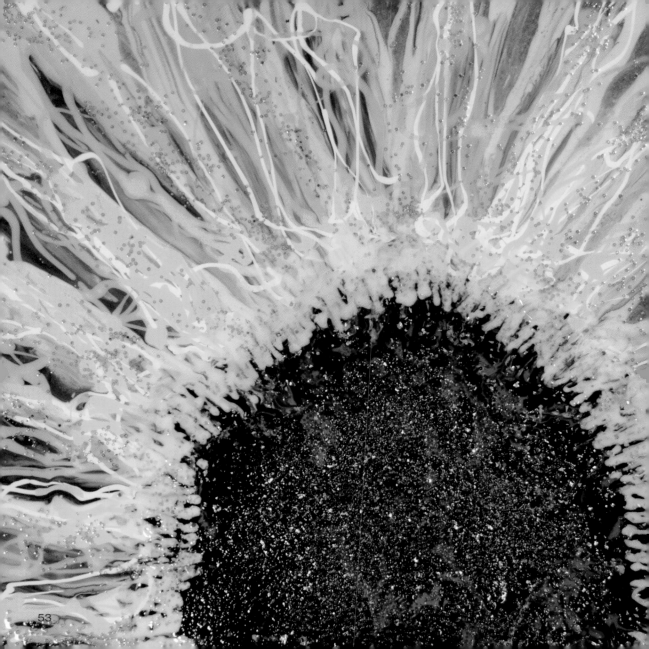

Painting Details

All paintings in this book are the creations of Peter W. Hart.

The inspiration for Peter's work comes from his emotions and energy. His themes are movement of colour and represent his immediate state of mind. The influence of day-to-day life is central to his art. It tells the story of his challenges, failures and successes using an array of strong and vivid colours to soft and warm hues.

Peter strives to be uniquely original by using multiple resources. His techniques include the use of different materials and media. The perspective of the abstract configuration is not representational of any subject but rather to let the viewer feel his energy and emotions.

You can view many of Peter's paintings at his gallery located at 367 Rue Saint Paul E. Montréal, QC H2Y 1H3 and online at www.PETERwHART.com.

"Hurricane of colors 1", 60" x 60", acrylic and mixed media on canvas, 2014 .... Cover

"Blue Energy 3", 18" x 24", acrylic on canvas, 2014 .... page 2

"A New Day", 24" x 48", acrylic on canvas, 2014 .... page 4

"Lava Meeting Water", 40" x 30", acrylic and mixed media on canvas, 2015 .... page 6

"Red Haven", 30" x 40", acrylic and mixed media on canvas, 2014 .... page 11

"Tradition", 40" x 30", acrylic and mixed media on canvas, 2015 .... page 12

"Rising Sunflower", 60" x 60", acrylic and mixed media on canvas, 2014 .... page 16

"Illusion", 24" x 36", acrylic and mixed media on canvas, 2014 .... page 21

"Nymphea", 16" x 20", acrylic on canvas, 2014... page 22

"New Season", 5½" x 6¼", acrylic and mixed media on canvas, 2014 .... page 26

"Maïa 1", 24" x 18", acrylic and mixed media on canvas, 2014 .... page 30

"Violet Rise 1", 72" x 48", acrylic and mixed media on canvas, 2014................................... page 34

"Once", 40" x 30", acrylic and mixed media on canvas, 2015 .... page 37

"Color Slide", 48" x 36", acrylic and mixed media on canvas, 2014 .... page 38

"Sea Storm", 24" x 48", acrylic and mixed media on canvas, 2014 .... page 32

"Summer Lane", 30" x 40", acrylic and mixed media on canvas, 2014.................................. page 46

"Hurricane of Colors 2", 60" x 60", acrylic and mixed media on canvas, 2014 .... page 49

"Ray", 24" x 36", acrylic and mixed media on canvas, 2014... page 53

"Happy Occasion", 30" x 40", acrylic and mixed media on canvas, 2015............................. page 56